Flowers On Kaleidoscope

High Contrast Kaleidoscopic Photos
Of Flowers To Color

ERIKA S. CLARK

In memory of my mother who taught me
the joy of growing flowers and food.

Copyright © 2012 Erika S. Clark

All rights reserved.

ISBN: 1535384301
ISBN-13: 978-153584308

Hydrangea
Rainbow Falls, South Carolina

Petunias

Shasta Daisy

Forget-Me-Not

Begonia

Cherry Blossoms

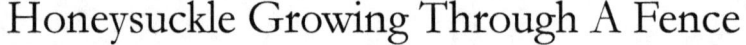
Honeysuckle Growing Through A Fence

Cosmos

Amaranthus

Zinnia with bee

Begonia

Petunia with butterfly

Chickweed

Phlox

White Rose of Sharon

Roses

Morning Glory

Monkey Grass

Monkey Grass

Myrtle

Petunias

Zinnia

Poppy

California Poppy

Portulaca

Zinnia

Myrtle

Rose of Sharon

Coneflower

Portulaca

Sunny Petunia

Rose of Sharon With Beautiful Green June Bug

Coneflower Center
Feed The Bees

Dwarf Iris

Mystery Flower
Bright Pink with two round petals and tiny yellow center

Wild Violets or Violas

Asiatic Lily

Zinnia Bud

ABOUT THE AUTHOR

Erika grew up with sand and sun in her hair in Narragansett, RI. Ever the adventurer and all around tiny animal finder, her interest in the small details and the humble parts of nature took hold.

She was set up on a blind date at 17-years-old where she found her husband. They raised three children in Groton, CT where their home was surrounded with woods and streams which helped nurture their kids' interest in nature.

Erika's background includes working as a CNA, MA(AAMA), and as a medical transcriptionist - which she enjoyed until she was replaced by a dragon.

Her continued love of nature, gardens, Beale Street Music Festival and her pets compels her to take far too many photos, some of which she would like to share.

A Note On The Format Change

Although this is an On Kaleidoscope coloring book, the format has been changed to allow for larger prints and thus a larger book size has been used. Image quality had unwittingly been sacrificed through the cropping process and the colorist deserves the best pages to personalize. Hopefully the coloring experience will be more harmonious with this setup.

Thank You.

www.ingramcontent.com/pod-product-compliance
Lightning Source LLC
Chambersburg PA
CBHW080721190526
45169CB00006B/2467